Cooking with Frozen (

Sandwiches, Appetizers, Main Dishes & More!

S. L. Watson

DEDICATION

To all the garlic lover's everywhere!

CONTENTS

Introduction

Oh how my family devours garlic bread! I love Texas toast garlic bread the best. We use frozen garlic bread 3 or 4 times a week. Garlic bread makes an ordinary sandwich or pizza so much more delicious. Open faced burgers and sloppy joes are quick and easy for dinner and so good on garlic bread. You can make unbelievable easy croutons, appetizers and snacks from garlic bread.

Besides being so delicious, how easy is it to place frozen garlic bread on a baking sheet. In a few minutes, the kitchen smells divine and everyone is ready to eat.

1 APPETIZERS

Garlic bread makes great crostini and bruschetta. My family devours them for parties, holidays and game day. They are so easy to make and everyone will love them.

Garlic Prosciutto Tapas

Makes 24 appetizer servings

8 slices frozen Texas Toast garlic bread
12 cherry tomatoes, halved
24 prosciutto slices
24 fresh parsley leaves

Preheat the oven to 400°. Place the garlic bread slices on a baking sheet. Bake for 8 minutes or until the bread is toasted. Remove the bread from the oven and cut each slice into 3 pieces. Top each slice with a tomato half, prosciutto slice and parsley leaf. Serve the tapas hot.

Garlic Crab Appetizers

Makes 4 dozen

12 slices frozen Texas Toast garlic bread
8 oz. American cheese, cubed
1/2 cup unsalted butter
1 lb. cooked crab meat
1 cup cooked chopped mushrooms

Preheat the oven to 400°. Place the garlic bread slices on a baking pan. Bake for 8 minutes or until the garlic bread is golden brown. Remove the bread from the oven. Leave the garlic bread on the baking pan.

In a sauce pan over low heat, add the American cheese and butter. Stir constantly and cook until the cheese melts. Remove the pan from the heat and stir in the crab meat and mushrooms.

Turn the oven to the broiler position. Spoon the cheese mixture over the garlic bread slices. Broil for 3 minutes or until the topping is bubbly and the garlic bread thoroughly heated. Remove the pan from the oven. Cut each garlic bread slice into 4 portions and serve.

Shrimp and Cheddar Toast

Makes 3 dozen appetizers

12 slices frozen Texas Toast garlic bread
2 cups shredded cheddar cheese
1 cup mayonnaise
1 cup finely chopped cooked shrimp
1/4 cup minced onion

Place the garlic bread on a baking pan. Preheat the oven to 350°. In a mixing bowl, add the cheddar cheese, mayonnaise, shrimp and onion. Stir until combined. Spread on the garlic bread.

Bake for 10 minutes or until the topping is bubbly and the garlic bread toasted. Remove the pan from the oven. Cut each garlic bread slice into 3 pieces and serve.

White Bean Black Olive Crostini

Makes 3 dozen

12 slices frozen Texas Toast garlic bread
2 cups cannellini beans, cooked
1/4 cup plus 1 tbs. olive oil
1/4 tsp. salt
1/4 tsp. black pepper
1/2 cup pitted kalamata olives, chopped
1/2 cup diced roasted red bell pepper
8 torn basil leaves

Preheat the 425°. Place the garlic bread slices on a baking sheet. Bake for 5 minutes or until the bread is toasted. Remove the bread from the oven.

In a food processor, add the cannellini beans, 1/4 cup olive oil, salt and black pepper. Process until smooth. In a small bowl, add the olives, red bell pepper and 1 tablespoon olive oil. Stir until well combined. Spread the bean mixture over the top of the garlic bread slices. Spoon a small dollop of the olive mixture over the bean puree. Sprinkle the bay leaves over the top. Cut each slice into 3 pieces and serve.

Tomato Goat Cheese Crostini

Makes 24 appetizer servings

8 slices frozen Texas Toast garlic bread
1/4 cup goat cheese
1/4 cup cream cheese, softened
5 plum tomatoes, chopped
2 tsp. chopped fresh herbs (use your favorite blend)

I like to use parsley, rosemary, thyme or basil for the herbs. Preheat the oven to 350°. Place the garlic bread slices on a baking sheet. Bake for 8 minutes or until the bread is toasted. Remove the bread from the oven.

In a mixing bowl, add the goat cheese, cream cheese, tomatoes and herbs. Stir until well combined. Spoon the spread on top of the slices. Cut each slice into 3 pieces and serve.

Fresh Tomato Onion Crostini

Makes 12 appetizer servings

16 oz. loaf frozen garlic bread, thawed
2 tbs. olive oil
1/2 tsp. salt
1/2 tsp. black pepper
3 cups tomato, finely chopped
1 cup finely chopped green onion
1/2 cup chopped parsley

Separate the bread into halves. Place the garlic bread on a baking sheet. Preheat the oven to 375°. Bake for 10 minutes or until the garlic bread is toasted and golden brown. Remove the garlic bread from the oven.

In a mixing bowl, add the olive oil, salt and black pepper. Whisk until combined. Add the tomato, green onion and parsley. Toss until combined and spoon over the garlic bread. Cut into slices and serve.

Almond Bacon Crostini

Makes 3 dozen

12 slices frozen Texas Toast garlic bread
2 bacon slices, cooked and crumbled
1 cup shredded Pepper Jack cheese
1/3 cup mayonnaise
1/4 cup sliced almonds, toasted
1 tbs. chopped green onions
1/4 tsp. salt

Preheat the oven to 400°. Line a baking sheet with aluminum foil. Place the garlic bread slices on the baking sheet. Bake for 8 minutes or until the bread is toasted. Remove the bread from the oven but leave the oven on.

In a mixing bowl, add the bacon, Pepper Jack cheese, mayonnaise, almonds, green onions and salt. Stir until well combined and spread on the garlic bread. Place the bread back in the oven for 5 minutes. Remove the pan from the oven. Cut each slice into 3 pieces and serve.

Swiss Blue Cheese Crostini

Makes 2 dozen

8 slices frozen Texas Toast garlic bread
12 oil packed sun dried tomatoes, halved
1 cup shredded Swiss cheese
4 oz. crumbled blue cheese
1/4 cup chopped fresh parsley

Line a baking sheet with aluminum foil. Preheat the oven to 400°. Place the garlic bread slices on the baking sheet. Bake for 8 minutes or until the bread is toasted. Remove the bread from the oven but leave the oven on. Cut each slice into 3 pieces.

Place a tomato half on each slice. In a small bowl, add the Swiss cheese, blue cheese and parsley. Stir until combined and spoon onto the bread slices. Bake for 5 minutes or until the cheeses melt. Remove the bread from the oven and serve.

Hot Artichoke Crostini

Makes 3 dozen

12 slices frozen Texas Toast garlic bread
1 cup mayonnaise
1 cup grated Parmesan cheese
14 oz. jar artichoke hearts, drained and chopped
4 oz. can diced green chiles, drained
2 garlic cloves, minced
1/2 cup finely chopped red bell pepper

Preheat the oven to 400°. Line a baking sheet with aluminum foil. Place the garlic bread slices on the baking sheet. Bake for 8 minutes or until the bread is toasted. Remove the bread from the oven but leave the oven on.

In a mixing bowl, add the mayonnaise, Parmesan cheese, artichokes, green chiles and garlic. Stir until well combined and spread on top of the garlic bread. Bake for 5 minutes. Remove the bread from the oven and sprinkle the red bell pepper over the top. Cut each slice into 3 pieces and serve.

Marinated Cheese Crostini

Makes 36 appetizers

1 lb. fresh mozzarella cheese
1 cup bottled olive oil vinaigrette
1 garlic clove, minced
1/4 tsp. black pepper
12 slices frozen Texas Toast garlic bread
18 cherry tomatoes, halved
Minced fresh basil, optional

Cut the mozzarella cheese into 1/4" thick slices and place in a shallow dish. You need 36 cheese slices for this recipe. In a mixing bowl, add the olive oil vinaigrette, garlic and black pepper. Whisk until well combined and pour over the mozzarella cheese. Cover the dish and refrigerate for 8 hours.

Place the garlic bread slices on a baking sheet. Preheat the oven to 350°. Bake for 8 minutes or until the bread is toasted. Remove the pan from the oven. Cut each slice into 3 pieces.

Drain all the liquid from the mozzarella cheese. Pat the cheese dry with a paper towel if desired. Place a mozzarella cheese slice on each garlic bread piece. Place a cherry tomato half on top and serve. Sprinkle fresh basil leaves over the top if desired.

Mozzarella Crostini

Makes 3 dozen

12 slices frozen Texas Toast garlic bread
Black pepper to taste
1/2 cup sliced green onions
6 Roma tomatoes, cut into 36 slices
1 1/2 cups shredded mozzarella cheese

Preheat the oven to 400°. Line a baking sheet with aluminum foil. Place the garlic bread slices on the baking sheet. Bake for 8 minutes or until the garlic bread is toasted. Remove the pan from the oven but leave the oven on. Sprinkle black pepper to taste over the garlic bread.

Sprinkle the green onions, tomatoes and mozzarella cheese over the bread. Bake for 5 minutes. Remove the pan from the oven. Cut each slice into 3 pieces and serve.

Spinach Crostini

Makes 8 appetizer servings

10 oz. pkg. frozen chopped spinach, thawed and drained
2 plum tomatoes, diced
1/2 cup diced onion
1 garlic clove, minced
1/2 cup crumbled feta cheese
1/4 cup mayonnaise
1/4 cup sour cream
1/4 tsp. black pepper
8 ct. pkg. frozen Texas Toast garlic bread

In a mixing bowl, add the spinach, tomatoes, onion, garlic, feta cheese, mayonnaise, sour cream and black pepper. Stir until well combined.

Preheat the oven to 350°. Spoon the spinach mixture on top of each garlic bread slice. Place the garlic bread on a baking sheet. Bake for 10 minutes or until the bread is golden brown and the topping hot. Remove the pan from the oven and serve.

Zucchini Feta Bruschetta

Makes 18 slices

1 tomato, seeded and chopped
1 zucchini, finely chopped
4 green onions, thinly sliced
2 tbs. minced fresh basil
4 garlic cloves, minced
2 tbs. lemon juice
2 tbs. olive oil
3/4 tsp. salt
1/4 tsp. black pepper
1/2 cup crumbled feta cheese
6 slices frozen Texas Toast garlic bread

In a mixing bowl, add the tomato, zucchini, green onions, basil and garlic. In a small bowl, add the lemon juice, olive oil, salt and black pepper. Stir until well combined and pour over the vegetables in the bowl. Toss until combined and add the feta cheese. Gently toss until combined. Cover the bowl and refrigerate for 1 hour.

Place the garlic bread slices on a baking sheet. Preheat the oven to 350°. Bake for 8 minutes or until the garlic bread is toasted and golden brown. Remove the bread from the oven.

Drain all the liquid from the vegetable mixture. Spoon the vegetable mixture over the garlic bread. Cut each slice into 3 pieces and serve.

Shrimp Bruschetta with Guacamole

Makes 12 appetizer servings

16 oz. loaf frozen garlic bread, thawed
2 large avocados, peeled and pitted
2 tsp. fresh lime juice
1/2 tsp. salt
1/4 tsp. ground cumin
3 garlic cloves, minced
1 tbs. diced onion
1/4 cup salsa
1/2 cup chopped fresh cilantro
1/4 cup olive oil
3/4 cup freshly grated Parmesan cheese

Separate the garlic bread into halves. Place the garlic bread on a large baking sheet. Preheat the oven to 375°. Bake for 12 minutes or until the garlic bread is toasted and golden brown. Remove the garlic bread from the oven.

In a mixing bowl, add the avocados, lime juice, salt, cumin, 1 garlic clove, onion, salsa and cilantro. Stir until combined. The avocados should still be in small chunks.

In a skillet over medium heat, add 2 garlic cloves and the olive oil. Saute the garlic for 2 minutes. Add the shrimp and cook only until the shrimp just begin to turn pink. The shrimp will not be completely cooked at this point. Remove the skillet from the heat.

Spoon the shrimp over the toasted garlic bread. Spoon a dollop of the guacamole over the shrimp. Sprinkle the Parmesan cheese over the top. Turn the oven to the broiler position. Broil for 4 minutes or until the shrimp are pink and the cheese melted. Remove from the oven. Cut into slices and serve.

Crab Bruschetta

Makes 16 appetizers

1/2 cup finely chopped shallots
2 garlic cloves, minced
2 tbs. olive oil
12 oz. lump crab meat, cooked
1 cup plum tomatoes, seeded and chopped
1 1/2 tsp. minced fresh basil
3/4 tsp. minced fresh oregano
8 slices frozen Texas Toast garlic bread

In a skillet over medium heat, add the shallots, garlic and olive oil. Saute the shallots and garlic for 5 minutes. Add the crab meat, tomatoes, basil and oregano to the skillet. Stir until combined and cook for 5 minutes. Remove the skillet from the heat.

Place the garlic bread on a baking sheet. Preheat the oven to 350°. Bake for 5 minutes or until the bread is toasted. Remove the bread from the oven.

Cut each garlic bread slice in half. Spoon the crab mixture over the top of each slice and serve.

Artichoke Spinach Dip Bruschetta

Makes 24 appetizers

16 oz. loaf frozen garlic bread, thawed
7 oz. jar marinated artichokes, drained and chopped
1/2 cup grated Romano cheese
1 plum tomato, seeded and chopped
1/3 cup finely chopped purple onion
1/3 cup fresh spinach, finely chopped
5 tbs. mayonnaise
1 garlic clove, minced

Preheat the oven to 400°. Place the garlic bread on a baking sheet. Separate the garlic bread into halves. Bake for 10 minutes or until the bread is toasted. Remove the bread from the oven.

In a mixing bowl, add the artichokes, Romano cheese, tomato, onion, spinach, mayonnaise and garlic. Stir until well combined. Spoon the mixture over the garlic bread. Bake for 5 minutes. Remove the bread from the oven. Cut into slices and serve.

Bacon Parmesan Crisps

Makes 1 dozen

16 oz. loaf frozen garlic bread, thawed
1/2 cup shredded Parmesan cheese
4 slices bacon, cooked and crumbled
Salt and black pepper to taste

Preheat the oven to 400°. Separate the garlic bread into halves. Place the garlic bread on a baking sheet. Bake for 10 minutes or until the bread is toasted. Remove the bread from the oven.

Sprinkle the Parmesan cheese and bacon over the bread. Season to taste with salt and black pepper. Bake for 5 minutes. Remove the bread from the oven. Cut into slices and serve.

Tomato Basil Toasts

Makes 12 servings

8 plum tomatoes, seeded and chopped
2 green onions, chopped
1 garlic clove, minced
1/4 cup balsamic vinegar
2 tbs. chopped fresh basil
2 tsp. olive oil
1/2 tsp. salt
1/2 tsp. black pepper
16 oz. loaf frozen garlic bread, thawed

In a mixing bowl, add the tomatoes, green onions, garlic, balsamic vinegar, basil, olive oil, salt and black pepper. Stir until combined. Cover the bowl and refrigerate for 1 hour.

Preheat the oven to 425°. Place the garlic bread on a baking sheet. Separate the garlic bread into halves. Bake for 10 minutes or until the bread is toasted. Remove the bread from the oven and cut into 12 slices. Spoon the tomato mixture onto the slices and serve.

2 SIDE DISHES & BREADS

Garlic bread is not only great as a side dish for a meal but it also make side dishes deliciously tasty. You can make an awesome salad and even fries from garlic bread.

Garlic Mushroom Stuffing

Makes 4 cups

8 slices frozen Texas Toast garlic bread
2/3 cup unsalted butter
1 cup chopped celery
1/2 cup chopped onion
6 cups sliced fresh mushrooms
1 tsp. dried sage
1 tsp. dried thyme
1 tsp. dried marjoram
1 tsp. poultry seasoning
1 tsp. salt
1/2 tsp. black pepper

Preheat the oven to 400°. Place the garlic bread slices on a baking sheet. Bake for 8 minutes or until the bread is toasted and golden brown. Remove the garlic bread from the oven and cool completely. Cut the bread into small pieces.

In a skillet over medium heat, add the butter, celery, onion and mushrooms. Saute the vegetables for 5 minutes. Add the garlic bread, sage, thyme, marjoram, poultry seasoning, salt and black pepper. Toss until well combined. Remove the skillet from the heat.

Preheat the oven to 325°. Spray a 9 x 13 casserole dish with non stick cooking spray. Spoon the stuffing into the casserole dish. Cover the dish with aluminum foil or a lid. Bake for 30 minutes. Remove the aluminum foil or lid from the stuffing. Bake for 15 minutes. Remove the stuffing from the oven and serve.

Garlic Bread Salad

Makes 4 servings

4 slices frozen Texas Toast garlic bread
2 plum tomatoes, sliced
1 cucumber, seeded and chopped
2 sliced green onions
2 tbs. shredded Parmesan cheese
4 cups chopped lettuce
3 tbs. red wine vinegar
1 garlic clove, minced
1/4 tsp. dried basil

Preheat the oven to 400°. Place the garlic bread slices on a baking pan. Bake for 8 minutes or until the garlic bread is golden brown. Remove the bread from the oven and cool completely. Cut the garlic bread into bite size pieces.

In a serving bowl, add the tomatoes, cucumber, green onion, Parmesan cheese and lettuce. In a small bowl, whisk together the red wine vinegar, garlic and basil. Pour the dressing over the salad. Toss until the salad is coated in the dressing. Add the garlic bread and toss until combined. Serve immediately.

Broccoli Corn Bake

Makes 6 servings

6 slices frozen Texas Toast garlic bread
10 oz. pkg. frozen chopped broccoli, thawed
15 oz. can whole kernel corn, drained
15 oz. can cream style corn

Preheat the oven to 375°. Place the garlic bread slices on a baking sheet. Bake for 8 minutes or until the garlic bread is well toasted and golden brown. Remove the garlic bread from the oven and cool for 10 minutes. Add the garlic bread to a food processor. Process until you have coarse crumbs.

Spray a 2 quart casserole dish with non stick cooking spray. Add the broccoli, whole kernel corn, cream style corn and 2/3 of the garlic bread crumbs to the casserole dish. Stir until combined. Bake for 15 minutes. Sprinkle the remaining garlic bread crumbs over the top of the casserole. Bake for 10 minutes or until the broccoli is tender. Remove the casserole from the oven and serve.

Garlic Parmesan Corn Casserole

Makes 12 servings

8 slices Texas Toast frozen garlic bread
1 1/2 cups whole milk
1 cup whipping cream
3 eggs
1/2 tsp. salt
1/2 tsp. black pepper
4 cups fresh corn kernels
1 1/2 cups shredded Parmesan cheese

Preheat the oven to 375°. Place the garlic bread slices on a baking sheet. Bake for 8 minutes or until the garlic bread is toasted and golden brown. Remove the garlic bread from the oven and cool for 5 minutes. Cut the garlic bread into bite size pieces.

In a mixing bowl, add the milk, whipping cream, eggs, salt and black pepper. Whisk until all the ingredients are well combined. Add the garlic bread to the mixing bowl and toss until the bread is moistened. Let the bread sit at room temperature for 30 minutes.

Preheat the oven to 375°. Add the corn and Parmesan cheese to the bowl. Stir until combined. Spray a 9 x 13 baking dish with non stick cooking spray. Spoon the casserole into the baking dish. Bake for 45 minutes or until the casserole is golden brown and set in the center. Remove the casserole from the oven and cool for 5 minutes before serving.

Bacon Cheddar Garlic Toast Fries

Makes 6 servings

8 slices frozen Texas Toast garlic bread
1 cup shredded cheddar cheese
1/2 cup thinly sliced green onion
1/4 cup crumbled cooked bacon

Cut the garlic bread into thin strips. Place the strips on a baking pan. Preheat the oven to 400°. Bake for 5 minutes. Sprinkle the cheddar cheese, green onion and bacon over the strips. Bake for 5 minutes or until the garlic bread strips are toasted and golden brown. Remove the pan from the oven and serve.

Cheeseburger Garlic Fries

Makes 6 servings

8 slices frozen Texas Toast garlic bread
1 lb. ground beef
8 American cheese slices
1/2 cup chopped onion
1 cup chopped tomato
1/4 cup chopped dill pickle
Salt and black pepper to taste

Cut the garlic bread into thin strips. Place the strips on a baking pan. Preheat the oven to 400°. Bake for 5 minutes. In a skillet over medium heat, add 1 lb. ground beef. Stir frequently to break the ground beef into crumbles as it cooks. Cook for 8 minutes or until the ground beef is no longer pink. Drain off any grease from the ground beef. Season the ground beef to taste with salt and black pepper.

Place the baked garlic bread fries on a baking sheet. Spoon the ground beef over the fries. Place the American cheese slices over the ground beef. Turn the oven to the broiler position. Broil for 3 minutes or until the cheese melts. Remove the pan from the oven.

Sprinkle the onion, tomato and dill pickle over the top and serve.

Garlic Toast Fries With Variations

Makes 6 servings

8 slices frozen Texas Toast garlic bread
1 cup warm marinara sauce

Cut the garlic bread into thin strips. Place the strips on a baking pan. Preheat the oven to 400°. Bake for 5 minutes or until the strips are crispy. Remove the fries from the oven and serve with marinara sauce. You can also fry the garlic bread in vegetable oil like french fries if desired. Garlic bread fries cook quickly in an air fryer.

There are endless variations for garlic bread fries. Use your imagination and I am sure you will come up with numerous ways to eat them.

Chili Cheese Fries: Heat a 15 oz. can Hormel chili with beans in the microwave. Pour over the fries and top with cheddar cheese.

Nacho Dipped Fries: Instead of using marinara sauce, use your favorite nacho cheese dip.

Garlic Fries with Dip: Substitute garlic fries for tortilla chips and serve with bean dip, spinach, artichoke or onion dip at your next party.

Garlic Fries with Hummus: Use garlic fries instead of chips with your favorite hummus. They are especially good with red pepper hummus.

Layered Garlic Bread Salad

Makes 6 servings

6 slices frozen Texas Toast garlic bread
6 green onions, chopped
1 green bell pepper, chopped
15 oz. can whole kernel corn, drained
15 oz. can black beans, drained
1/2 cup prepared ranch dressing
1/2 cup salsa
2 diced tomatoes
1 cup shredded cheddar cheese

Preheat the oven to 400°. Place the garlic bread slices on a baking pan. Bake for 8 minutes or until the garlic bread is toasted and golden brown. Remove the garlic bread from the oven and cool completely. Cut the garlic bread into bite size pieces.

Place the garlic bread in a large serving bowl. Sprinkle the green onions and green bell pepper over the garlic bread. Spoon the corn over the top. Spoon the black beans over the corn. In a small bowl, stir together the ranch dressing and salsa. Pour the dressing over the top of the salad. Sprinkle the tomatoes and cheddar cheese over the top and serve.

Italian Garlic Bread Salad

Makes 8 servings

8 slices frozen Texas Toast garlic bread
6 cups chopped tomatoes
1 cup minced fresh basil
1 cup thinly sliced purple onion
1/2 cup olive oil
2 tbs. red wine vinegar
1/2 tsp. salt
1/2 tsp. black pepper
1 garlic clove, minced

Preheat the oven to 400°. Place the garlic bread slices on a baking sheet. Bake for 8 minutes or until the bread is toasted and golden brown. Remove the bread from the oven and cool completely.

Cut the bread into bite size pieces. Add the garlic bread, tomatoes, basil and onion to a serving bowl. In a small bowl, whisk together the olive oil, red wine vinegar, salt, black pepper and garlic. Pour the dressing over the salad. Let the salad sit for 20 minutes at room temperature. Serve immediately.

Italian Stuffed Mushrooms

Makes 30 mushrooms

3 slices frozen Texas Toast garlic bread
4 bacon slices, diced
30 large fresh button mushrooms
1/4 lb. cooked ground ham
1 cup shredded mozzarella cheese
1/4 cup grated Parmesan cheese
1 tomato, finely chopped
2 tbs. minced fresh parsley
1/2 tsp. dried oregano

Preheat the oven to 400°. Place the garlic bread on a baking pan. Bake for 8 minutes or until the garlic bread is toasted and golden brown. Remove the bread from the oven and cool for 10 minutes. Add the garlic bread to a food processor. Process until you have coarse crumbs.

In a skillet over medium heat, add the bacon. Cook for 8 minutes or until the bacon is crispy. Remove the skillet from the heat. Remove the stems from the mushrooms. Finely chop half the stems and add to a mixing bowl. Discard the remaining stems. Add the garlic bread crumbs to the mixing bowl.

Crumble the bacon and add to the bowl. Add the ham, mozzarella cheese, Parmesan cheese, tomato, parsley and oregano. Stir until combined. Spoon the filling into the mushroom caps. Place the mushrooms on a baking sheet.

Preheat the oven to 425°. Bake for 15 minutes. Remove the mushrooms from the oven and serve.

Black Olive Herb Garlic Bread

Makes 12 servings

16 oz. loaf frozen garlic bread, thawed
1/3 cup chopped black olives
1/2 cup chopped fresh parsley
1/3 cup chopped green onions
1 1/2 tsp. dried basil
1/2 tsp. dried tarragon

Preheat the oven to 350°. Separate the garlic bread into halves. In a small bowl, add the black olives, parsley, green onions, basil and tarragon. Stir until well combined and spread on the cut side of each bread half. Place the halves together and wrap the bread in aluminum foil.

Bake for 25 minutes or until the bread is toasted. Remove the bread from the oven and cut into slices to serve.

Creamy Garlic Bread

Makes 8 servings

8 oz. cream cheese, softened
1/4 cup sour cream
1/4 cup grated Parmesan cheese
2 tbs. mayonnaise
2 tbs. minced fresh parsley
1 tbs. minced green onion
8 slices frozen Texas Toast garlic bread

In a small bowl, add the cream cheese, sour cream, Parmesan cheese, mayonnaise, parsley and green onion. Stir until combined. Preheat the oven to 450°. Spread the cream cheese on one side of each garlic bread slice. Place the garlic bread slices on a baking pan. Bake for 8 minutes or until the topping is bubbly and the garlic bread golden brown. Remove the bread from the oven and serve.

Pizza Pesto Bread

Makes 8 servings

8 slices frozen Texas Toast garlic bread
1/2 cup olive oil
4 garlic cloves, peeled
1 1/2 cups fresh basil leaves
2 cups shredded provolone cheese

Preheat the oven to 400°. Place the garlic bread slices on a baking sheet. Bake for 5 minutes. Remove the bread from the oven but leave the oven on.

In a food processor, add the olive oil, garlic and basil. Process until smooth and combined. Spread the pesto on one side of each garlic bread slice. Sprinkle the provolone cheese over the pesto. Bake for 5 minutes or until the cheese melts and the garlic bread is golden brown. Remove the pan from the oven and serve.

Herb French Bread

Makes 8 servings

1/4 cup grated Parmesan cheese
1 tsp. dried basil
1 tsp. dried rosemary
16 oz. loaf frozen garlic bread, thawed

In a small bowl, add the Parmesan cheese, basil and rosemary. Stir until combined. Separate the garlic bread into halves. Spoon the Parmesan cheese mixture over the bread.

Preheat the oven to 425°. Place the bread on a baking sheet. Bake for 10 minutes or until the bread is toasted and golden brown. Remove the bread from the oven and serve.

Herb Vegetable Garlic Cheese Bread

Makes 8 servings

8 frozen Texas Toast garlic bread slices
1 cup shredded mozzarella cheese
1/2 cup grated carrot
2 green onions, sliced
1/2 tsp. dried Italian seasoning
1/4 cup mayonnaise

Preheat the oven to 400°. Place the garlic bread slices on a baking sheet. In a small bowl, add the mozzarella cheese, carrot, green onions, Italian seasoning and mayonnaise. Stir until well combined and spread on one side of each bread slice.

Bake for 15 minutes or until the bread is golden brown and the topping hot and bubbly. Remove the bread from the oven and serve hot.

Cayenne Garlic Bread

Makes 6 servings

16 oz. loaf frozen garlic bread, thawed
3 tbs. grated Parmesan cheese
1/4 tsp. black pepper
1/4 tsp. cayenne pepper
2 drops Tabasco sauce

Separate the garlic bread into two halves. Preheat the oven to 350°. Place the garlic bread on a baking sheet. In a small bowl, add the Parmesan cheese, black pepper, cayenne pepper and Tabasco sauce. Stir until well combined and spread over the garlic bread.

Bake for 10-12 minutes or until the bread is toasted and the Parmesan cheese melted. Remove the bread from the oven and cut into slices. Serve hot.

I like to turn this bread into a shrimp sandwich. Pile cooked spicy shrimp on top of the bread and cut into open face sandwiches. Roast beef is also very good on this bread.

Greek Garlic Bread

Makes 8 slices

16 oz. loaf frozen garlic bread, thawed
2 tbs. mayonnaise
1/2 cup cooked sliced mushrooms
1/2 cup sliced black olives
2 tbs. chopped green onion tops
1 cup shredded mozzarella cheese

Preheat the oven to 400°. Separate the garlic bread into halves. In a mixing bowl, stir together the mayonnaise, mushrooms, olives and green onions. Stir until well combined and spread on the garlic bread.

Preheat the oven to 400°. Place a large sheet of aluminum foil on a baking sheet. Place the garlic bread on the baking sheet. Sprinkle the mozzarella cheese over the top of the bread. Wrap each half in aluminum foil. Bake for 20 minutes or until the bread is hot and the cheese melted. Remove the bread from the oven. Remove the bread from the aluminum foil. Cut into slices and serve.

Mexican Cheesy Garlic Bread

Makes 6 servings

16 oz. loaf frozen garlic bread, thawed
8 oz. pkg. shredded Mexican cheese blend
1 1/2 tsp. dried parsley flakes
1/4 tsp. ground cumin

Separate the garlic bread into halves. In a small bowl, add the Mexican cheese blend, parsley and cumin. Stir until combined and sprinkle on the garlic bread.

Preheat the oven to 350°. Place the garlic bread on a baking sheet. Bake for 15 minutes or until the cheese is melted and the bread toasted. Remove the baking sheet from the oven and cut the bread into slices. Serve hot.

Dill Garlic Bread

Makes 8 servings

16 oz. loaf frozen garlic bread, thawed
1/4 cup grated Parmesan cheese
1/4 cup finely chopped fresh dill

Separate the garlic bread into halves. Sprinkle the Parmesan cheese and dill over the top of the bread.

Preheat the oven to 350°. Place the garlic bread on a baking sheet. Bake for 10 minutes or until the cheese is melted and the bread toasted. Remove the baking sheet from the oven. Cut the bread into slices and serve.

Garlic Pesto Bread

Makes 6 servings

16 oz. loaf frozen garlic bread, thawed
3 oz. softened cream cheese
1/2 cup refrigerated basil pesto
1 cup finely diced tomatoes

Preheat the oven to 400°. Separate the garlic bread into halves. Place the garlic bread on a baking sheet. Bake for 10 minutes or until the garlic bread is toasted. Remove the garlic bread from the oven,

In a small bowl, add the cream cheese and pesto. Stir until combined and spread over the garlic bread. Bake for 2 minutes. Remove the garlic bread from the oven and sprinkle the tomatoes over the top. Cut into slices and serve.

Cheesy Bacon Onion Garlic Bread

Makes 8 servings

8 slices frozen Texas Toast garlic bread
8 oz. bacon, cooked and crumbled
1/2 cup chopped onion
1 1/2 cups shredded cheddar cheese

Preheat the oven to 350°. Place the garlic bread slices in a 9 x 13 casserole dish. Sprinkle the bacon and onion over the top of the bread. Sprinkle the cheddar cheese over the top.

Bake for 20 minutes or until the garlic bread is toasted and the cheddar cheese bubbly. Remove the dish from the oven and serve.

Sicilian Garlic Bread

Makes 8 servings

16 oz. loaf frozen garlic bread, thawed
5 oz. pkg. grated Romano cheese
1/4 tsp. black pepper

Separate the garlic bread into halves. Sprinkle the Romano cheese and black pepper over the bread.

Preheat the oven to 350°. Wrap each bread half in aluminum foil. Place the bread on a baking sheet. Bake for 25 minutes. Remove the bread from the oven. Cut the bread into slices to serve.

Potato Crusted Garlic Texas Toast

Makes 8 servings

3 eggs
1/2 cup whole milk
1/2 tsp. dried thyme
1/2 tsp. salt
1/8 tsp. black pepper
3 green onions, finely chopped
Dash of Tabasco sauce
8 slices frozen garlic Texas Toast
2 cups instant potato flakes
6 tbs. unsalted butter

In a mixing bowl, add the eggs, milk, thyme, salt, black pepper, green onions and Tabasco sauce. Whisk until well combined. Place the potato flakes in a shallow dish. Dip the bread slices in the egg mixture allowing the excess egg to drip off back into the bowl. Dredge the bread slices in the potato flakes.

In a large skillet over medium heat, add the butter. When the butter melts and is hot, add the garlic bread. Cook about 3 minutes on each side or until the bread is golden brown and toasted. Remove the bread from the skillet and serve hot.

Savory Mushroom Toast

Makes 4 servings

2 cups sliced fresh mushrooms
1/4 cup unsalted butter
2 garlic cloves, minced
1 tsp. lemon juice
1/2 tsp. salt
1/8 tsp. black pepper
8 slices Texas Toast frozen garlic bread, toasted

In a skillet over medium heat, add the mushrooms and butter. Saute the mushrooms for 5 minutes. Add the garlic cloves and saute the garlic for 2 minutes. Add the lemon juice, salt and black pepper to the skillet. Stir until combined and cook for 1 minute. Remove the skillet from the heat.

Place the garlic toast on a serving platter. Spoon the mushrooms over the toast and serve.

Easy Garlic Croutons

Makes about 6 cups

8 slices frozen Texas Toast garlic bread

Thaw the garlic bread for 3 minutes at room temperature. With a sharp knife, cut the bread into bite size pieces. Place the croutons, in a single layer, on a large baking sheet. Preheat the oven to 400°. Bake for 10 minutes or until the croutons are golden brown and toasted. Remove the croutons from the oven and cool for 10 minutes before serving.

These are great in salads and soups. Store leftovers covered in the refrigerator. Reheat in the oven to crisp up leftover croutons.

Spicy Garlic Croutons

Makes about 4 cups

6 slices frozen Texas Toast garlic bread
2 tbs. olive oil
2 tsp. chili powder
1 tsp. salt
1 tsp. black pepper

Preheat the oven to 375°. Place the garlic bread slices on a baking sheet. Bake for 5 minutes. Remove the bread from the oven and cool for 5 minutes. Cut the garlic bread into small pieces.

In a mixing bowl, add the garlic bread, olive oil, chili powder, salt and black pepper. Toss until combined. Spread the croutons, in a single layer, on the baking sheet. Bake for 15 minutes or until the croutons are golden brown. Stir the croutons occasionally while baking. Remove the croutons from the oven and cool for 10 minutes before using.

Rosemary Garlic Croutons

Makes about 4 cups

6 slices frozen Texas Toast garlic bread
2 tsp. chopped fresh rosemary
1/2 tsp. black pepper
3 tbs. olive oil
2 tbs. freshly grated Parmesan cheese

Preheat the oven to 375°. Place the garlic bread slices on a baking sheet. Bake for 5 minutes. Remove the bread from the oven and cool for 5 minutes. Cut the garlic bread into small pieces.

In a mixing bowl, add the garlic bread, rosemary, black pepper, olive oil and Parmesan cheese. Toss until combined. Spread the croutons, in a single layer, on the baking sheet. Bake for 15 minutes or until the croutons are golden brown. Stir the croutons occasionally while baking. Remove the croutons from the oven and cool for 10 minutes before using.

Garlic Breadcrumb Mix

Use for coating chicken, turkey, pork chops and cheese sticks. Make wonderful breadcrumbs for topping casseroles.

Makes 2 cups

8 slices frozen Texas Toast garlic bread
1/3 cup grated Parmesan cheese
1 tsp. dried parsley flakes
1/2 tsp. black pepper

Preheat the oven to 400°. Place the garlic bread slices on a baking sheet. Bake for 10 minutes or until the bread is golden brown and toasted. Make sure the bread is well toasted for crumbs. Remove the bread from the oven and cool completely.

Add the garlic bread to a food processor. Process until you have fine crumbs. Pour the crumbs into a bowl. Add the Parmesan cheese, parsley flakes and black pepper to the bowl. Stir until combined. Store the breadcrumb mix in an airtight container in the refrigerator up to 1 month.

3 MAIN DISHES & SANDWICHES

Garlic bread is fabulous used in casseroles, main dishes, sandwiches and for pizza. Garlic bread adds another dimension of flavor to your dish.

Scrambled Egg Casserole

Makes 4 servings

4 slices frozen Texas Toast garlic bread
2 tbs. unsalted butter
8 eggs, beaten
1 cup whole milk
8 oz. American cheese, cubed
1 cup cooked diced ham

Preheat the oven to 375°. Place the garlic bread slices on a baking pan. Bake for 8 minutes or until the garlic bread is toasted and well browned. Remove the garlic bread from the oven. Cool for 5 minutes and cut the garlic bread into bite size pieces.

In a skillet over medium heat, add the butter. When the butter melts, add the eggs. Stir constantly and cook for 5 minutes scrambling the eggs. The eggs should be done but still moist when ready. Remove the skillet from the heat.

In a sauce pan over medium heat, add the milk and American cheese. Stir constantly and cook until the cheese melts. Remove the pan from the heat and stir in the eggs and ham.

Spray an 8" square baking pan with non stick cooking spray. Add the garlic bread to the baking pan. Pour the egg mixture over the top. Bake for 20 minutes or until the casserole is set and hot. Remove the dish from the oven and serve.

Beefy Garlic Nachos

Makes 8 servings

1 lb. ground beef
14 oz. can diced tomatoes
15 oz. can chili beans in sauce
1 cup sliced black olives
6 green onions, sliced
1 tbs. chili powder
12 frozen Texas Toast garlic bread slices
2 cups shredded cheddar cheese

In a skillet over medium heat, add the ground beef. Stir frequently to break the ground beef into crumbles as it cooks. Cook for 8 minutes or until the ground beef is well browned and no longer pink. Drain all the grease from the skillet.

Add the tomatoes with juice, chili beans with sauce, black olives, green onions and chili powder to the skillet. Stir until well combined and bring the beef to a boil. Reduce the heat to low. Stir occasionally and simmer for 20 minutes. Remove the skillet from the heat.

While the ground beef is cooking, bake the garlic bread. Preheat the oven to 400°. Place the garlic bread on a baking pan. Bake for 8 minutes or until the garlic bread is well toasted and golden brown. Remove the garlic bread from the oven and cool for 5 minutes. Cut the garlic bread into bite size pieces.

Place the garlic bread on a serving platter. Spoon the ground beef over the garlic bread. Sprinkle the cheddar cheese over the top and serve.

Sausage Gumbo Pie

Makes 10 servings

1 lb. smoked sausage, cut into 1/4" thick slices
1 green bell pepper, chopped
1 cup chopped onion
1/4 cup instant roux mix
10 oz. can diced tomatoes with green chiles
4 cups chicken broth
16 oz. pkg. frozen sliced okra
1 cup dry instant rice
1/2 tsp. Cajun seasoning
1/2 tsp. dried thyme
12 slices frozen Texas Toast garlic bread

In a dutch oven over medium heat, add the smoked sausage, green bell pepper and onion. Saute for 8 minutes. Add the roux mix to the pan. Stir constantly and cook for 2 minutes. Add the tomatoes with juice, chicken broth, okra, rice, Cajun seasoning and thyme. Stir constantly and bring the gumbo to a boil. Cook for 1 minute and remove the pan from the heat.

Preheat the oven to 425°. Place the garlic bread slices in a 9 x 13 casserole dish. You may have to cut the slices to make them fit. Make sure the bottom of the dish is covered. Bake for 4 minutes. Remove the bread from the oven. Spoon the gumbo over the bread. Cover the dish with a lid or aluminum foil. Bake for 10 minutes. Remove the lid or aluminum foil. Bake for 10 minutes or until the bread is toasted and the rice tender. Remove the pie from the oven and serve.

Garlic Taco Pie

Makes 6 servings

6 slices frozen Texas Toast garlic bread
1 lb. ground beef
11 oz. can Mexicorn, drained
1 cup tomato sauce
1 envelope dry taco seasoning mix
1 cup shredded cheddar cheese

Preheat the oven to 400°. Place the garlic bread slices in a 9" pie pan. Cut the slices to fit if needed to form a crust. Bake for 5 minutes. Remove the bread from the oven.

In a skillet over medium heat, add the ground beef. Stir frequently to break the ground beef into crumbles as it cooks. Cook for 8 minutes or until the ground beef is well browned and no longer pink. Drain off any excess grease. Stir in the Mexicorn, tomato sauce and taco seasoning mix. Stir constantly and cook for 5 minutes. Remove the skillet from the heat. Spoon the taco filling over the garlic bread slices. Sprinkle the cheddar cheese over the top.

Bake for 10 minutes or until the garlic bread is golden brown and the cheese melted. Remove the pie from the oven and serve.

Saucy Beef Casserole

Makes 4 servings

1 lb. ground beef
1 cup chopped onion
10.75 oz. can cream of chicken soup
10.75 oz. can condensed vegetable soup
4 frozen Texas Toast garlic bread slices

In a skillet over medium heat, add the ground beef and onion. Stir frequently to break the ground beef into crumbles as it cooks. Cook for 8 minutes or until the ground beef is well browned and no longer pink. Drain off any excess grease. Add the cream of chicken soup and vegetable soup to the skillet. Stir until combined and bring the soups to a boil. When the soups are boiling, remove the skillet from the heat.

Preheat the oven to 350°. Spoon the ground beef into an 8" square baking pan. Cover the pan with aluminum foil for a lid. Bake for 20 minutes. Remove the lid or aluminum foil. Place the garlic bread slices over the top of the dish. Bake for 15 minutes or until the garlic bread is toasted. You may need to turn the garlic bread over halfway through the baking time. Remove the casserole from the oven and serve.

Spinach Stuffed Garlic Toast

Makes 12 servings

4 cups shredded mozzarella cheese
15 oz. carton ricotta cheese
10 oz. pkg. frozen chopped spinach, thawed and drained
12 slices frozen Texas Toast garlic bread
3 cups spaghetti sauce

In a mixing bowl, add the mozzarella cheese, ricotta cheese and spinach. Stir until combined. Preheat the oven to 350°. Place the garlic bread slices on a baking sheet. Spread the spinach mixture over the garlic bread slices.

Bake for 15 minutes. Spread the spaghetti sauce over the top of the garlic bread. Bake for 10 minutes or until the garlic bread is toasted and the cheeses bubbly. Remove the bread from the oven and serve.

Vegetable Ham Casserole

Makes a 11 x 7 casserole

1 1/2 cups sliced fresh mushrooms
1 1/2 cups chopped zucchini
1 cup diced cooked ham
3/4 cup chopped onion
3/4 cup chopped green bell pepper
1 garlic clove, minced
2 tbs. vegetable oil
8 oz. cream cheese, softened
1/4 cup half and half
6 eggs
4 slices frozen Texas Toast garlic bread, thawed
1 1/2 cups shredded cheddar cheese
1/2 tsp. salt
1/4 tsp. black pepper

In a large skillet over medium heat, add the mushrooms, zucchini, ham, onion, green bell pepper, garlic and vegetable oil. Saute the vegetables for 8 minutes or until they are tender. Remove the skillet from the heat and drain off any liquid.

In a mixing bowl, add the cream cheese and half and half. Using a mixer on medium speed, beat until smooth and combined. Add the eggs and mix until combined. Turn the mixer off. Add the vegetables to the bowl and stir until combined.

Preheat the oven to 350°. Place the garlic bread slices on a baking pan. Bake for 8 minutes or until the garlic bread is toasted and golden brown. Remove the garlic bread from the oven and cool for 5 minutes. Cut the garlic bread into bite size pieces.

Add the garlic bread, cheddar cheese, salt and black pepper to the bowl. Stir until well combined. Spray a 11 x 7 casserole dish with non stick cooking spray. Spoon the casserole into the dish. Bake for 35 minutes or until a knife inserted in the center of the casserole comes out clean. Remove the dish from the oven and serve.

Garlic Bread Spaghetti Casserole

Makes 8 servings

8 slices frozen Texas Toast garlic bread
26 oz. jar spaghetti sauce
2 cups chopped green bell pepper
14 oz. can diced tomatoes, drained
8 oz. ricotta cheese
8 oz. can sliced mushrooms, drained
1/2 cup chopped onion
3 garlic cloves, minced
12 fresh basil leaves, minced
1/2 tsp. dried oregano
3 cups shredded mozzarella cheese

Preheat the oven to 400°. Place the garlic bread slices on a baking pan. Bake for 8 minutes or until the garlic bread is well toasted and golden brown. Remove the garlic bread from the oven. Cool the bread completely. Cut the garlic bread into bite size pieces.

Spray a 9 x 13 casserole dish with non stick cooking spray. In a mixing bowl, add the spaghetti sauce, green bell pepper, tomatoes, ricotta cheese, mushrooms, onion, garlic, basil, oregano and 1 1/2 cups mozzarella cheese. Stir until well combined. Add the garlic bread pieces and toss until combined. Spoon the casserole into the dish. Sprinkle 1 1/2 cups mozzarella cheese over the top.

Bake for 30 minutes or until the casserole is hot and bubbly. Remove the dish from the oven and cool for 5 minutes before serving.

Creole Tuna Cakes

Makes 8 cakes

4 slices frozen Texas Toast garlic bread
2 cans drained solid white tuna, 12 oz. size
2 eggs
2 tsp. grated lemon zest
1/3 cup plus 2 tsp. mayonnaise
1 tsp. Creole seasoning
2 tbs. vegetable oil

Preheat the oven to 375°. Place the garlic bread slices on a baking sheet. Bake for 8 minutes or until the garlic bread is well toasted and golden brown. Remove the bread from the oven and cool completely. Add the garlic bread to a food processor. Process until you have fine crumbs. You need 1 1/4 cups crumbs for this recipe. Save any remaining crumbs for another recipe.

In a mixing bowl, add the garlic breadcrumbs, tuna, eggs, lemon zest, mayonnaise and Creole seasoning. Stir until well combined. Form the tuna into 8 patties.

In a skillet over medium heat, add 1 tablespoon vegetable oil. When the oil is hot, add 4 tuna patties. Cook for 3 minutes on each side or until they are golden brown. Remove the patties from the skillet. Add the remaining vegetable oil and cook the remaining tuna patties. Serve hot.

Baked Garlic Tomato Pie

Makes a 9" pie

6 slices frozen Texas Toast garlic bread
3 tomatoes, cut into 1/4" slices
10 bacon slices, cooked and crumbled
1 cup shredded cheddar cheese
1 cup mayonnaise

Preheat the oven to 350°. Place the garlic bread slices in a 9" pie pan to form a crust. You may need to cut the bread to fit the pie pan. Bake for 2 minutes. Remove the pie from the oven. Place the tomatoes over the garlic bread.

In a small bowl, add the cheddar cheese and mayonnaise. Stir until combined and spread over the tomatoes. Bake for 15 minutes or until the garlic bread is toasted, golden brown and the cheese melted. Remove the pie from the oven and serve.

Beefy Garlic Bread Pizza Bake

Makes 8 servings

10 slices frozen Texas Toast garlic bread, thawed
1 lb. ground beef
15 oz. jar pizza sauce
1 cup chopped green bell pepper
1 cup chopped onion
2 cups sliced fresh mushrooms
3 oz. sliced pepperoni
1 cup shredded mozzarella cheese
1 cup shredded cheddar cheese

Cut the garlic bread into bite size pieces. Spray a 9 x 13 casserole dish with non stick cooking spray. Place the garlic bread in the casserole dish. In a skillet over medium heat, add the ground beef. Stir frequently to break the ground beef into crumbles as it cooks. Cook for 8 minutes or until the ground beef is well browned and no longer pink. Remove the skillet from the heat.

Spread the pizza sauce over the garlic bread in the dish. Spoon the ground beef over the sauce. Sprinkle the green bell pepper, onion, mushrooms and pepperoni over the top of the sauce. Sprinkle the mozzarella and cheddar cheese over the top of the casserole. Bake for 30 minutes or until the garlic bread is toasted and the casserole hot. Remove the dish from the oven and cool for 5 minutes before serving.

Chicken Pepperoni Pizza

Makes 4 servings

16 oz. loaf frozen garlic bread, thawed
3/4 cup pizza sauce
1 cup frozen chopped broccoli, thawed
1 cup cubed cooked chicken
4 oz. can sliced mushrooms, drained
1/4 cup sliced pepperoni
8 cherry tomatoes, halved
1 1/2 cups shredded mozzarella cheese

Separate the garlic bread into halves. Place the garlic bread on a baking sheet. Spread the pizza sauce over the garlic bread. Place the broccoli, chicken, mushrooms, pepperoni and tomatoes over the garlic bread.

Preheat the oven to 400°. Bake for 10 minutes. Sprinkle the mozzarella cheese over the top of the pizza. Bake for 5 minutes or until the garlic bread is toasted and the cheese melted. Remove the pizza from the oven and serve.

Chicken Alfredo Pizza

Makes 4 servings

16 oz. loaf frozen garlic bread, thawed
10 oz. container refrigerated Alfredo sauce
10 oz. pkg. frozen spinach, thawed and drained
1 cup diced cooked chicken
1 cup chopped tomato
1/2 cup cooked and crumbled bacon

Preheat the oven to 400°. Separate the garlic bread into halves. Place the garlic bread on a baking sheet. Spread the Alfredo sauce over the garlic bread. Squeeze all the water from the spinach. Pat the spinach dry with paper towels if needed.

Place the spinach and chicken over the garlic bread. Bake for 15 minutes or until the garlic bread is toasted. Remove the pizza from the oven. Sprinkle the tomato and bacon over the top and serve.

Chicken Parmesan Pizza

This is so easy and everyone loves it!

Makes 4 servings

16 oz. loaf frozen garlic bread, thawed
8 frozen cooked chicken tenders (Tyson)
1/2 cup pizza sauce
1 cup shredded Parmesan cheese
2 tbs. chopped fresh basil

Preheat the oven to 375°. Separate the garlic bread into halves and place on a baking sheet. Place the chicken tenders on a baking sheet. Bake for 10 minutes or until the garlic bread is toasted and the chicken tenders hot. Remove the garlic bread and chicken from the oven.

Spread the pizza sauce over the garlic bread. Place the chicken tenders over the sauce. Sprinkle the Parmesan cheese over the top of the chicken. Bake for 5 minutes or until the cheese melts. Remove the pizza from the oven and sprinkle the basil over the top. Cut into slices and serve.

Cheddar Ham Breakfast Sandwiches

Makes 4 servings

4 slices frozen Texas Toast garlic bread, thawed
1 1/2 tsp. dried basil
1/2 tsp. dried rosemary
1 1/2 cups finely diced ham
1 1/2 cups shredded cheddar cheese

Preheat the oven to 400°. Place the garlic bread on a baking sheet. Sprinkle the basil and rosemary over the garlic bread. Sprinkle the ham and cheddar cheese over the bread. Bake for 10 minutes or until the garlic bread is golden brown and the cheese melted. Remove the pan from the oven and serve.

Ham & Swiss Brunch Casserole

Makes a 9 x 13 baking pan

16 oz. loaf frozen garlic bread, thawed
8 oz. thinly sliced cooked ham
8 oz. thinly sliced Swiss cheese
4 eggs
2 cups whole milk
1/4 cup grated Parmesan cheese
1/4 cup dry breadcrumbs
2 tbs. chopped fresh parsley
3 tbs. melted unsalted butter

Separate the garlic bread into halves. Cut the garlic bread into 1/2" slices. Place half the garlic bread slices in the bottom of a 9 x 13 baking pan. The slices will overlap. Place the ham and Swiss cheese slices over the bread. Place the remaining bread slices over the ham and cheese.

In a mixing bowl, add the eggs and milk. Whisk until combined and pour over the top of the dish. In a small bowl, stir together the Parmesan cheese, breadcrumbs, parsley and butter. Sprinkle over the top of the dish.

Preheat the oven to 375°. Bake for 35 minutes or until the casserole is puffed and golden brown. Remove the casserole from the oven and cool for 5 minutes before serving.

Garlic Sausage Casserole

Makes 6 servings

6 slices frozen Texas Toast garlic bread
1 lb. ground pork sausage
3/4 cup shredded Swiss cheese
3 eggs
1 tsp. prepared yellow mustard
1 1/4 cups whole milk
2/3 cup half and half
1/8 tsp. black pepper

Spray a 9 x 13 casserole dish with non stick cooking spray. Preheat the oven to 350°. Place the garlic bread slices on a baking pan. Bake for 5 minutes. Remove the bread from the oven and cool while you prepare the rest of the dish. Leave the oven on.

In a skillet over medium heat, add the sausage. Stir frequently to break the sausage into crumbles as it cooks. Cook for 8 minutes or until the sausage is well browned and no longer pink. Remove the skillet from the heat and drain all the grease from the sausage.

Cut the garlic bread into bite size pieces and place in the casserole dish. Sprinkle the sausage over the garlic bread. Sprinkle the Swiss cheese over the garlic bread. In a mixing bowl, add the eggs, mustard, milk, half and half and black pepper. Whisk until combined and pour over the bread.

Bake for 25 minutes or until a knife inserted in the center of the casserole comes out clean. Remove the casserole from the oven and serve.

Mushroom Stacks

Makes 8 servings

6 cups chopped fresh mushrooms
2 jalapeno peppers, seeded and chopped
1 tbs. olive oil
1/4 cup minced fresh cilantro
8 slices frozen Texas Toast garlic bread
2 cups shredded Monterey Jack cheese

In a skillet over medium heat, add the mushrooms, jalapeno peppers and olive oil. Saute the vegetables for 8 minutes or until they are tender. Add the cilantro and cook for 1 minute. Remove the skillet from the heat.

Preheat the oven to 400°. Place the garlic bread slices on a baking pan. Bake for 4 minutes. Remove the bread from the oven. Spoon the mushrooms over the top of the garlic bread slices. Sprinkle the Monterey Jack cheese over the mushrooms. Bake for 4 minutes or until the garlic bread is golden brown and the cheese melted. Remove the pan from the oven and serve.

Italian Sausage Garlic Bread Pizza

Makes 4 servings

1 lb. ground Italian sausage
1 tbs. olive oil
1 onion, thinly sliced
1 cup pizza sauce
1 1/2 tsp. dried oregano
1/4 tsp. crushed red pepper flakes
1/4 tsp. salt
16 oz. loaf frozen garlic bread, thawed
2/3 cup ricotta cheese
2 cups shredded mozzarella cheese
1/4 cup grated Parmesan cheese

In a skillet over medium heat, add the Italian sausage. Stir frequently and break the sausage into crumbles as it cooks. Cook about 8 minutes or until the sausage is no longer pink and well browned. Remove the skillet from the heat and drain all the grease from the sausage.

Remove the sausage from the skillet and set aside. Add the olive oil and onion to the skillet. Saute the onion for 5 minutes. Remove the skillet from the heat and stir in the pizza sauce. Add the sausage to the skillet along with the oregano, red pepper flakes and salt. Stir until well combined.

Separate the garlic bread into halves. Spread the ricotta cheese over the top of the garlic bread. Spoon the sausage mixture over the garlic bread. Sprinkle the mozzarella cheese and Parmesan cheese over the top.

Place the garlic bread on the baking sheet. Bake for 15 minutes or until the cheeses are melted and the bread hot and toasted. Remove the pizza from the oven and cut into slices to serve.

Mexican Cheese Steak Sandwiches

Makes 4 servings

1 1/2 lb. flank steak
1 envelope dry taco seasoning mix
6 tbs. melted unsalted butter
1 1/2 tsp. lime juice
1 garlic clove, minced
1/4 cup water
16 oz. loaf frozen garlic bread, thawed
2 tbs. olive oil
1 onion, thinly sliced
1 green bell pepper, thinly sliced
1 red bell pepper, thinly sliced
8 oz. jar cheese dip
4 oz. can chopped green chiles, drained

Cut the flank steak, across the grain, into thin strips. In a Ziploc bag, add the taco seasoning mix, 3 tablespoons butter, lime juice, garlic, water and steak strips. Close the bag and shake until all the ingredients are well combined. Refrigerate the steak for 1 hour.

Preheat the oven to 400°. Separate the garlic bread into halves. Place the garlic bread on a baking sheet. Bake for 15 minutes or until the garlic bread is toasted. Remove the garlic bread from the oven.

In a skillet over medium heat, add the olive oil. When the oil is hot, add the onion, green bell pepper and red bell pepper. Saute the vegetables for 6 minutes or until they are tender. Remove the vegetables from the skillet.

Add 3 tablespoons butter to the skillet. Drain the marinade from the steak and discard the marinade. Add the steak to the skillet. Cook for 4 minutes or until the steak is done to your taste.

Spoon the steak onto one half of the garlic bread. Spoon the onion and peppers over the steak. Microwave the cheese sauce until hot. Spoon the cheese sauce over the top of the steak and vegetables. Spoon the green chiles over the top of the cheese sauce. Place the remaining half of the garlic bread over the sandwich. Cut into slices and serve.

Italian Meatloaf Sandwiches

Makes 6 sandwiches

1 1/2 lb. lean ground beef
3/4 cup quick cooking oats
3/4 cup whole milk
1/4 cup chopped onion
1 egg, beaten
1 1/2 tsp. salt
1/4 tsp. black pepper
1/3 cup ketchup
2 tbs. light brown sugar
1 tbs. yellow prepared mustard
16 oz. loaf frozen garlic bread, thawed
1 cup spaghetti sauce
2 cups shredded Italian cheese blend

In a mixing bowl, add the ground beef, oats, milk, onion, egg, salt and black pepper. Using your hands, mix until combined. Pat the meat into a 9 x 5 loaf pan. In a small bowl, add the ketchup, brown sugar and mustard. Stir until combined and spread over the meatloaf.

Preheat the oven to 350°. Bake for 1 hour or until the meatloaf is no longer pink. Remove the pan from the oven and drain off any excess grease. Cool the meatloaf for 10 minutes.

Place the garlic bread on a baking sheet. Separate the garlic bread into halves. Bake for 10 minutes or until the bread just begins to brown. Remove the bread from the oven. Cut the meatloaf into 8 slices. Place the slices on one half of the garlic bread. You will have to overlap the slices. Spread the spaghetti sauce over the meatloaf. Sprinkle the Italian cheese blend over the top. Place the remaining half of garlic bread over the sandwich. Bake for 15 minutes or until the garlic bread is toasted and the cheese bubbly. Remove the sandwich from the oven and serve.

Basil Tomato Meatloaf Sandwiches

Makes 8 sandwiches

1 1/2 lb. lean ground beef
3/4 cup quick cooking oats
3/4 cup whole milk
1/4 cup chopped onion
1 egg, beaten
1 1/2 tsp. salt
1/4 tsp. black pepper
1/3 cup ketchup
2 tbs. light brown sugar
1 tbs. yellow prepared mustard
8 slices frozen Texas Toast garlic bread
1/2 cup mayonnaise
1 tbs. chopped fresh basil
1 cup shredded lettuce
2 plum tomatoes, sliced

In a mixing bowl, add the ground beef, oats, milk, onion, egg, salt and black pepper. Using your hands, mix until combined. Pat the meat into a 9 x 5 loaf pan. In a small bowl, add the ketchup, brown sugar and mustard. Stir until combined and spread over the meatloaf.

Preheat the oven to 350°. Bake for 1 hour or until the meatloaf is no longer pink. Remove the pan from the oven and drain off any excess grease. Cool the meatloaf for 10 minutes.

Place the garlic bread on a baking sheet. Bake for 8 minutes or until the bread is golden brown. Remove the bread from the oven. In a small bowl, add the mayonnaise and basil. Stir until combined and spread on one side of each piece of garlic bread. Sprinkle the lettuce over mayonnaise. Place the tomatoes over the lettuce. Cut the meatloaf into 8 slices. Place a slice over each bread slice and serve.

Marinated Steak Sandwiches

Makes 6 sandwiches

1 cup dry red wine
3 tbs. soy sauce
1 tbs. minced garlic
1/8 tsp. black pepper
2 flank steaks, 1 lb. each
2 tbs. olive oil
6 slices frozen Texas Toast garlic bread
2 cups diced tomatoes
3 cups chopped lettuce

In a Ziploc bag, add the red wine, soy sauce, garlic, black pepper and flank steaks. Close the bag and shake until the marinade is combined and the steaks are coated in the marinade. Refrigerate the steaks at least 2 hours but not more than 12 hours.

Remove the steaks from the bag. Discard the marinade. In a skillet over medium high heat, add the olive oil. When the oil is hot, add the flank steaks. Cook for 3 minutes on each side or until the steaks are cooked to your taste. Remove the skillet from the heat. Let the steaks rest for 5 minutes.

Preheat the oven to 400°. Place the garlic bread slices on a baking sheet. Bake for 5 minutes or until the garlic bread is golden brown. Remove the pan from the oven.

Place the garlic bread slices on a serving platter. Thinly slice the steaks across the grain. Place the steak slices over the garlic bread. Sprinkle the tomatoes and lettuce over the top and serve.

Caramelized Onion Beef Sandwiches

Makes 4 sandwiches

1 tsp. salt
1/4 tsp. garlic powder
1/4 tsp. paprika
1/4 tsp. black pepper
1 lb. beef tenderloin
3 tbs. unsalted butter
1 tbs. vegetable oil
2 tbs. light brown sugar
3 onions, peeled and thinly sliced
2 tbs. water
8 slices frozen Texas Toast garlic bread
1 1/2 cups fresh baby spinach

Preheat the oven to 450°. In a small bowl, add 1/2 teaspoon salt, garlic powder, paprika and black pepper. Stir until combined and rub over the beef tenderloin. Place the beef tenderloin in a roasting pan. Bake for 30 minutes or until the tenderloin is done to your taste. Remove the tenderloin from the oven and cool while you prepare the onions. Leave the oven on.

In a large skillet over medium heat, add the butter and vegetable oil. When the oil is hot, add the brown sugar, 1/2 teaspoon salt, onions and water. Stir frequently and cook for 15 minutes. The onions should be lightly caramelized when ready. Remove the skillet from the heat.

While the onions are cooking, bake the garlic bread. Place the garlic bread slices on a baking sheet. Bake for 5-7 minutes or until the garlic bread is golden brown. Remove the garlic bread from the oven.

Thinly slice the beef tenderloin and place the slices over 4 garlic bread slices. Spoon the onions over the beef. Sprinkle the spinach over the onions. Place the remaining garlic bread slices over the sandwiches and serve.

Cheese Steak Melts

Makes 4 servings

16 oz. loaf frozen garlic bread, thawed
2 cups shredded mozzarella cheese
1 lb. thinly sliced deli roast beef
1 tsp. Montreal steak seasoning
1 1/2 cups thinly sliced onions
1 1/2 cups thinly sliced green bell peppers

Preheat the oven to 400°. Separate the garlic bread into halves. Place the garlic bread on a baking sheet. Sprinkle the mozzarella cheese over one garlic bread half. Place the roast beef slices over the cheese. Sprinkle the Montreal steak seasoning over the roast beef. Sprinkle the onions and green bell peppers over the roast beef. Place the remaining garlic bread half over the top of the sandwich.

Wrap the garlic bread in aluminum foil. Bake for 30 minutes or until the garlic bread is toasted and the onions and peppers tender. Remove the sandwich from the oven. Cut into slices and serve.

Smothered Beef Sandwiches

Makes 6 sandwiches

16 oz. loaf frozen garlic bread, thawed
3 cups cooked diced roast beef
1/2 cup barbecue sauce
1 1/2 cups shredded American cheese

Preheat the oven to 375°. Separate the garlic bread into halves. In a small bowl, add the roast beef and barbecue sauce. Stir until combined and spoon over the garlic bread. Bake for 10 minutes or until the garlic bread is toasted. Sprinkle the American cheese over the top. Bake for 5 minutes or until the cheese melts. Remove the garlic bread from the oven. Cut into slices and serve.

Beef Stroganoff Sandwiches

Makes 8 servings

1 1/2 lbs. ground beef
1 cup chopped onion
2 garlic cloves, minced
2 tbs. all purpose flour
1/2 tsp. salt
1/2 tsp. paprika
10.75 oz. can cream of mushroom soup
1/2 cup sliced fresh mushrooms
8 slices frozen Texas Toast garlic bread

In a skillet over medium heat, add the ground beef, onion and garlic. Stir frequently to break the ground beef into crumbles as it cooks. Cook for 8 minutes or until the ground beef is well browned and no longer pink. Drain off any excess grease.

Add the all purpose flour, salt and paprika to the skillet. Stir constantly and cook for 2 minutes. Add the cream of mushroom soup and mushrooms. Stir until combined and simmer for 5 minutes. The stroganoff should be hot and bubbly. Remove the skillet from the heat.

While the ground beef is cooking, bake the garlic bread. Preheat the oven to 400°. Place the garlic bread slices on a baking pan. Bake for 8 minutes or until the garlic bread is toasted and golden brown. Remove the garlic bread from the oven.

Place the garlic bread on a serving platter. Spoon the stroganoff over the top and serve.

Garlic Sloppy Joes

Makes 6 servings

1 lb. lean ground beef
1/2 cup chopped onion
1/2 cup chopped green bell pepper
14 oz. can fire roasted diced tomatoes with garlic
1/2 cup ketchup
1 tsp. chili powder
1 tsp. Worcestershire sauce
1/4 tsp. salt
1/8 tsp. black pepper
6 frozen Texas Toast garlic bread slices
6 slices provolone cheese, 1 oz. each

In a skillet over medium heat, add the ground beef, onion and green bell pepper. Stir frequently to break the ground beef into crumbles as it cooks. Cook for 10 minutes or until the ground beef is no longer pink and well browned. Drain off any grease from the ground beef.

Add the tomatoes with juice, ketchup, chili powder, Worcestershire sauce, salt and black pepper to the skillet. Stir constantly and cook for 5 minutes. Remove the skillet from the heat.

While the ground beef is cooking, bake the garlic bread. Preheat the oven to 400°. Place the garlic bread slices on a baking sheet. Bake for 7 minutes or until the garlic bread is golden brown and toasted. Remove the garlic bread from the oven. Spoon the ground beef over the garlic bread. Place a provolone cheese slice over each serving.

Turn the oven to the broiler position. Broil for 2 minutes or until the cheese is melted and bubbly. Remove the sandwiches from the oven and serve.

Italian Burgers

Makes 4 burgers

1 cup tomato sauce
1/4 tsp. dried basil
1/4 tsp. dried red pepper flakes
1/8 tsp. garlic powder
1 lb. ground Italian sausage
1 thinly sliced onion
8 slices mozzarella cheese, 1 oz. each
8 slices frozen Texas Toast garlic bread

In a sauce pan over medium heat, add the tomato sauce, basil, red pepper flakes and garlic powder. Stir until combined and bring the sauce to a boil. When the sauce is boiling, reduce the heat to low. Stir occasionally and simmer the sauce for 10 minutes. Remove the pan from the heat.

Form the Italian sausage into 4 patties. In a skillet over medium heat, add the patties. Cook for 5 minutes on each side or until the burgers are well browned and no longer pink. Remove the burgers from the skillet.

Add the onion to the skillet. Cook for 6 minutes or until the onion is tender. Remove the skillet from the heat. Preheat the oven to 400°. Place the garlic bread slices on a baking pan. Place a mozzarella cheese slice over each piece of garlic bread. Bake for 6 minutes or until the garlic bread is toasted. Remove the bread from the oven. Place a burger on 4 garlic bread slices. Spoon the onions over the burgers. Spoon the sauce to taste over the burgers. Place the remaining garlic bread slices over the sandwiches and serve.

I like to spoon a small amount of sauce over the burgers and serve the rest with the burgers.

Antipasto Po' Boys

Makes 4 servings

16 oz. loaf frozen garlic bread, thawed
1/4 cup creamy Parmesan salad dressing
2 tbs. grated Parmesan cheese
14 oz. can artichoke hearts, drained and chopped
1 cup diced tomatoes
5 oz. pkg. thinly sliced pepperoni
1/2 cup sliced black olives
1 cup shredded mozzarella cheese

Preheat the oven to 400°. Separate the garlic bread into halves. Place the garlic bread on a baking pan. Bake for 4 minutes. Remove the bread from the oven.

In a mixing bowl, add the Parmesan salad dressing, Parmesan cheese, artichokes and tomatoes. Stir until combined and spread over the garlic bread. Place the pepperoni over the garlic bread. Sprinkle the black olives and mozzarella cheese over the garlic bread.

Bake for 10 minutes or until the garlic bread is toasted. Remove the bread from the oven. Place one half of the garlic bread over the other half. Cut into slices and serve.

Roasted Vegetable Sandwiches

Makes 4 servings

1 medium eggplant, peeled
1 tsp. salt
2 zucchini, cut into 1/4" thick slices
3 yellow squash, cut into 1/4" thick slices
1 red bell pepper, cut into 1/2" strips
1 onion, peeled and halved
3 tbs. olive oil
1/2 tsp. black pepper
3 tbs. chopped fresh basil
1 tbs. chopped fresh parsley
16 oz. loaf frozen garlic bread, thawed
4 provolone cheese slices

Cut the eggplant into 1/4" thick slices. Place the eggplant slices on paper towels. Sprinkle 1/2 teaspoon salt over the eggplant. Let the eggplant slices sit at room temperature for 20 minutes.

In a mixing bowl, add the eggplant, zucchini, yellow squash and red bell pepper. Cut the onion into 1/4" thick slices and add to the bowl. Sprinkle 1/2 teaspoon salt over the vegetables. Add the olive oil and black pepper to the bowl. Toss until the vegetables are coated in the olive oil.

Preheat the oven to 450°. Place the vegetables, in a single layer, on a large baking sheet. Bake for 20 minutes or until the vegetables are tender. Remove the vegetables from the oven and sprinkle the basil and parsley over the vegetables. Toss until combined.

Separate the garlic bread into halves. Place the vegetables on one garlic bread half. Place the provolone cheese slices over the top of the vegetables. Place the remaining garlic bread half over the top. Wrap the sandwich in aluminum foil. Bake for 30 minutes or until the garlic bread is toasted and the cheese melted. Remove the sandwich from the oven and serve.

Cajun Shrimp Sandwich

Makes 6 servings

1 cup unsalted butter
2 onions, chopped
1 1/2 tsp. minced garlic
1 tsp. Creole seasoning
3 lbs. fresh shrimp, peeled and deveined
16 oz. loaf frozen garlic bread, thawed

In a large dutch oven over medium heat, add the butter. When the butter melts, add the onions, garlic and Creole seasoning. Saute the onions and garlic for 6 minutes or until the vegetables are tender. Add the shrimp and stir until combined. Place a lid on the pan and cook for 8 minutes or until the shrimp turn pink. Remove the pan from the heat.

While the shrimp are cooking, toast the bread. Separate the garlic bread into halves. Place the garlic bread on a baking sheet. Preheat the oven to 350°. Bake the bread for 8 minutes or until the bread is toasted. Remove the bread from the oven and place on a serving platter. Spoon the shrimp over the garlic bread. Cut into slices and serve.

Shrimp Avocado Sandwiches

Makes 4 servings

4 bacon slices
1 lb. fresh shrimp, peeled and deveined
1/2 tsp. salt
1/4 tsp. black pepper
1/4 cup fresh lemon juice
1 1/2 cups cherry tomatoes, halved
5 oz. pkg. fresh arugula
1 cup fresh corn kernels
1/4 cup thinly sliced purple onion
1 tbs. olive oil
4 frozen Texas Toast garlic bread slices
2 tbs. mayonnaise
2 avocados, peeled and sliced
Salt and black pepper to taste

In a skillet over medium heat, add the bacon. Cook for 8 minutes or until the bacon is crispy. Remove the bacon from the skillet and drain on paper towels. Add the shrimp to the skillet. Sprinkle 1/2 teaspoon salt over the shrimp. Cook for 4 minutes or until the shrimp turn pink. Remove the skillet from the heat. Add the black pepper and lemon juice to the skillet. Toss until the shrimp are coated in the lemon juice.

In a mixing bowl, add the cherry tomatoes, arugula, corn, purple onion and olive oil. Toss until combined. Season to taste with salt and black pepper.

Preheat the oven to 400°. Place the garlic bread slices on a baking sheet. Bake for 5 minutes or until the bread is toasted. Remove the garlic bread from the oven and place on a serving platter. Crumble the bacon.

Spread the mayonnaise over one side of the garlic bread. Place the bacon, shrimp and avocados over the mayonnaise. Spoon the arugula salad over the top and serve.

Garlic Tuna Melts

Makes 4 servings

12 oz. can albacore tuna, drained
4 tbs. finely chopped onion
4 tbs. finely chopped green bell pepper
2 tbs. finely chopped dill pickles
4 tbs. mayonnaise
1/2 cup shredded cheddar cheese
8 slices frozen Texas Toast garlic bread, thawed

In a mixing bowl, add the tuna, onion, green bell pepper, pickles and mayonnaise. Stir until combined. Preheat the oven to 400°. Place the garlic bread slices on a baking pan. Spread the tuna salad over 4 of the bread slices. Sprinkle the cheddar cheese over the top of the tuna. Place the remaining bread slices over the top.

Bake for 15 minutes or until the garlic bread is toasted and the cheese melted. Remove the sandwiches from the oven and serve.

Cheesy Garlic Chicken Sandwiches

Makes 4 servings

1 lb. boneless skinless chicken breast, cut into thin strips
1 envelope dry Caesar salad dressing mix
2 tbs. olive oil
1 cup sliced fresh mushrooms
1/2 cup sliced purple onion
4 slices frozen Texas Toast garlic bread
4 slices provolone cheese

Add the chicken to a mixing bowl. Sprinkle the Caesar dressing mix over the chicken. Toss until the chicken is coated in the seasonings. In a skillet over medium heat, add the olive oil. When the oil is hot, add the mushrooms and purple onion. Saute the vegetables for 5 minutes. Remove the vegetables from the skillet and set aside.

Add the chicken to the skillet. Cook for 6 minutes or until the chicken is no longer pink and tender. Remove the skillet from the heat. Preheat the oven to 350°. Place the garlic bread slices on a baking pan. Bake for 3 minutes.

Spoon the chicken and vegetables over the top of the garlic bread. Place a provolone cheese slice over each sandwich. Bake for 5 minutes or until the garlic bread is toasted and the cheese melted. Remove the sandwiches from the oven and serve.

Open Face Buffalo Chicken Sandwiches

Makes 6 sandwiches

6 frozen Texas Toast garlic bread slices
4 cups cooked shredded chicken
1/4 tsp. garlic powder
1/8 tsp. salt
1/8 tsp. black pepper
1/4 cup Tabasco sauce
1/4 cup unsalted butter
1 tbs. honey
2 cups thinly sliced cucumbers
1/2 cup prepared ranch dressing

Preheat the oven to 450°. Place the garlic bread slices on a baking pan. Bake for 5-7 minutes or until the garlic bread is toasted and golden brown. Remove the bread from the oven.

While the garlic bread is baking, add the chicken, garlic powder, salt, black pepper, Tabasco sauce, butter and honey to a skillet over medium heat. Stir constantly and cook for 5 minutes or until the butter melts and the chicken is hot. Remove the skillet from the heat.

Place the garlic bread slices on a serving platter. Spoon the chicken over the garlic bread. Place the cucumber slices over the chicken. Drizzle the ranch dressing over the top and serve.

Meatball Sandwich

Makes 6 servings

1 lb. ground beef
1 lb. ground pork sausage
2 cups spaghetti sauce
16 oz. loaf frozen garlic bread, thawed
6 oz. sliced provolone cheese

In a mixing bowl, add the ground beef and sausage. Use your hands and mix until the meats are combined. Form the meat into 1" meatballs. In a skillet over medium heat, add the meatballs. Cook the meatballs about 10 minutes or until the meatballs are well browned and no longer pink. Remove the skillet from the heat. Drain off the excess drippings. Remove the meatballs from the skillet and drain on paper towels.

Add the spaghetti sauce to the skillet. Add the meatballs back to the skillet. Stir constantly and cook for 5 minutes. Remove the skillet from the heat.

Separate the garlic bread into halves. Preheat the oven to 450°. Place the garlic bread on a baking sheet. Bake for 8 minutes or until the bread is golden brown and toasted. Remove the bread from the oven. Spoon the meatballs and sauce over the bread. Place the provolone cheese over the top.

Turn the oven to the broiler position. Broil for 3 minutes or until the cheese is hot and bubbly. Remove the sandwiches from the oven and serve.

Garlic Shrimp Open Face Po' Boys

Makes 4 servings

3 cups water
12 oz. fresh shrimp, peeled and deveined
2 tbs. finely chopped green onions
8 frozen Texas Toast garlic slices, toasted
8 slices bacon, cooked crisp
8 tomato slices, about 1/4" thick
Salt and black pepper to season

Add the water to a large sauce pan over medium heat. When the water is boiling, add the shrimp. Cook the shrimp about 4 minutes or until they turn pink. Remove the pan from the heat and drain all the water from the shrimp. Rinse the shrimp in cold water until they are chilled. Drain all the water from the shrimp. Pat the shrimp dry with paper towels if needed.

Refrigerate the shrimp until well chilled. When the shrimp are chilled, chop the shrimp into small pieces. Place the shrimp in a mixing bowl and add the green onions. Toss until well combined.

Spread the shrimp on one side of 4 garlic bread slices. Place 2 bacon slices and 2 tomato slices over the shrimp. Season to taste with salt and black pepper. Place the remaining garlic bread slices over the top and serve.

Prosciutto Tomato Sandwiches

Makes 4 sandwiches

8 slices frozen Texas Toast garlic bread
1/3 cup mayonnaise
1/4 cup crumbled blue cheese
2 cups arugula
4 oz. pkg. thinly sliced prosciutto
1 large tomato, cut into 4 slices
Black pepper to taste

Preheat the oven to 400°. Place the garlic bread slices on a baking sheet. Bake for 5 minutes or until the bread is toasted. Remove the pan from the oven. In a small bowl, stir together the mayonnaise and blue cheese. Spread the mixture on one side of each bread slice.

Place the arugula, prosciutto and tomato slices over the mayonnaise on 4 slices. Season to taste with black pepper. Place the remaining slices over the top and serve.

Texas Toast Tomato Sandwiches

Makes 6 servings

6 slices frozen Texas Toast garlic bread
6 tomatoes, sliced
1/3 cup bottled blue cheese vinaigrette dressing
6 tbs. chopped fresh basil
1/2 cup crumbled blue cheese
Salt and black pepper to taste

Preheat the oven to 375°. Place the garlic bread on a baking sheet. Bake for 8 minutes or until the garlic bread is toasted and golden brown. Remove the garlic bread from the oven.

Place the garlic bread slices on a serving platter. Place the tomato slices over the bread. Season to taste with salt and black pepper. Drizzle the blue cheese dressing over the tomatoes. Sprinkle the basil and blue cheese over the tomatoes and serve.

Grilled Garlic Vegetable Sandwiches

Makes 4 servings

2 zucchini, cut into 1/2" slices
1 purple onion, cut into 1/4" slices
2 red bell peppers, seeded and halved
3 oz. goat cheese, softened
3 oz. pkg. cream cheese, softened
1 garlic clove, minced
1 tbs. crushed fresh rosemary
8 slices Texas Toast frozen garlic bread, toasted

Have your indoor or outdoor grill hot and ready. Spray the grill with non stick cooking spray. Place the zucchini, purple onion and red bell peppers on the grill. Grill the vegetables for 6 minutes or until the vegetables are tender. Remove the vegetables from the grill.

In a small bowl, add the goat cheese, cream cheese, garlic and rosemary. Stir until combined. Spread the mixture on one side of the garlic bread slices. Place the vegetables over the cheese spread. Place the remaining bread slices over the vegetables and serve.

Fresh Spinach & Bacon Sandwiches

Makes 6 servings

1 1/2 lbs. fresh spinach
3/4 cup softened cream cheese
3/4 tsp. black pepper
1/4 tsp. salt
12 slices frozen Texas Toast garlic bread slices, toasted
8 oz. bacon, cooked and crumbled

Remove the stems from the spinach and finely chop the spinach. In a small bowl, add the cream cheese, black pepper and salt. Stir until combined and spread on one side of each bread slice.

Place the spinach and bacon over 6 bread slices. Place the remaining slices over the top of the sandwiches and serve.

Cheesy Spinach Bacon Sandwiches

Makes 4 servings

16 oz. loaf frozen garlic bread, thawed
3 garlic cloves, minced
2 tbs. olive oil
16 oz. pkg. frozen chopped spinach, thawed
3/4 tsp. salt
1/4 tsp. black pepper
6 bacon slices, cooked and crumbled
1 1/2 cups shredded mozzarella cheese
1/4 cup shredded Parmesan cheese

Preheat the oven to 400°. Separate the garlic bread into halves. Place the garlic bread on a baking sheet. Bake for 4 minutes. Remove the bread from the oven.

In a skillet over medium heat, add the garlic and olive oil. Saute the garlic for 2 minutes. Add the spinach, salt and black pepper to the skillet. Saute the spinach for 4 minutes. Remove the skillet from the heat and stir in the bacon. Spoon the spinach over the garlic bread.

Sprinkle the mozzarella and Parmesan cheese over the spinach. Bake for 5 minutes or until the garlic bread is toasted and the cheeses melted. Remove the bread from the oven. Cut into slices and serve.

Fried Eggplant Sandwiches

Makes 8 servings

2 small eggplants, peeled
2 cups Italian seasoned breadcrumbs
3/4 cup grated Parmesan cheese
3 eggs
3 tbs. water
3 tbs. olive oil
2 loaves thawed frozen garlic bread, 16 oz. size
2 cups spaghetti sauce
1 cup shredded mozzarella cheese

Slice the eggplant into 1/2" slices. In a shallow bowl, add the Italian breadcrumbs and Parmesan cheese. Stir until combined. Add the eggs and water to a shallow dish. Whisk until smooth and well combined.

Preheat the oven to the broiler position. Spray two baking sheets with non stick cooking spray. Dip each eggplant slice in the egg wash allowing the excess egg to drip off back into the bowl. Dredge each eggplant slice in the breadcrumb mixture. Place the eggplant slices on a baking sheet. Brush the olive oil over the eggplant slices. Broil the eggplant about 5 minutes on each side or until the eggplant is tender. Remove the eggplant from the oven. Leave the broiler on.

Separate the garlic bread into halves. Place the garlic bread on a baking sheet. Preheat the oven to 400°. Bake for 15 minutes or until the bread is toasted and golden brown. Place the eggplant slices over the garlic bread. Spread the spaghetti sauce over the eggplant. Sprinkle the mozzarella cheese over the sauce. Preheat the oven to the broiler position. Broil for 3 minutes or until the cheese is melted and bubbly. Remove the bread from the oven. Cut into slices and serve.

Three Cheese Tomato Melt

Makes 4 servings

8 slices frozen Texas Toast garlic bread
1/2 cup shredded cheddar cheese
1/4 cup shredded mozzarella cheese
2 tbs. grated Parmesan cheese
4 tbs. mayonnaise
8 tomato slices, 1/2" thick

Preheat the oven to 400°. Place the garlic bread on a baking pan. Bake for 3 minutes. Remove the bread from the oven. In a small bowl, add the cheddar cheese, mozzarella cheese, Parmesan cheese and mayonnaise.

Place a tomato slice over each piece of garlic bread. Spread the cheese mixture over the top of the tomatoes. Bake for 5 minutes or until the garlic bread is toasted and the topping bubbly. Remove the sandwiches from the oven and serve.

Baked Turkey Southwestern Sandwiches

Makes 8 servings

1 cup chopped black olives
1/2 tsp. chili powder
1/2 tsp. ground cumin
1/4 tsp. salt
1/2 cup mayonnaise
1/3 cup sour cream
1/3 cup chopped green onion
8 slices frozen Texas Toast garlic bread
1 lb. thinly sliced cooked turkey
8 tomato slices
2 ripe avocados, peeled and sliced
3/4 cup shredded cheddar cheese
3/4 cup Monterey Jack cheese

In a small bowl, add the black olives, chili powder, cumin, salt, mayonnaise, sour cream and green onion. Stir until combined. Preheat the oven to 400°. Place the garlic bread slices on a baking sheet. Bake for 4 minutes. Remove the bread from the oven.

Place the turkey slices over the garlic bread. Place a tomato slice over the turkey. Place the avocado slices over the tomatoes. Spread the black olive mixture over the top. Sprinkle the cheddar and Monterey Jack cheese over the top of the sandwiches. Bake for 5 minutes or until the garlic bread is toasted and the cheeses melted. Remove the sandwiches from the oven and serve.

Cheddar Guacamole Burgers

Makes 4 burgers

1 lb. ground beef
1 1/2 tsp. salt
1/4 tsp. black pepper
2 ripe avocados, pitted and peeled
1 tbs. grated onion
1 tbs. lemon juice
1/3 cup mayonnaise
4 bacon slices, cooked and crumbled
4 slices cheddar cheese, 1 oz. each
4 slices frozen Texas Toast garlic bread

In a mixing bowl, add the ground beef, 1/2 teaspoon salt and black pepper. Mix until combined and form the meat into 8 thin patties. In a mixing bowl, add the avocados, 1 teaspoon salt, onion, lemon juice, mayonnaise and bacon. Stir until smooth and combined. Spoon the avocado mixture in the center of 4 burger patties. Place the remaining patties over the filling. Pinch the edges together until sealed.

In a skillet over medium heat, add the burgers. Cook about 6 minutes on each side or until the burgers are no longer pink. Place a cheddar cheese slice over each burger. Remove the skillet from the heat. While the burgers are cooking, bake the garlic bread. Preheat the oven to 400°. Place the garlic bread slices on a baking sheet. Bake for 8 minutes or until the garlic bread is toasted and golden brown. Remove the garlic bread from the oven.

Place a burger over each garlic bread slice and serve.

Po' Boy Cheeseburgers

Makes 8 servings

1 lb. lean ground beef
1/2 cup crushed garlic croutons
1/2 cup whipping cream
1/4 cup ketchup
1/4 cup chopped onion
1 tbs. Worcestershire sauce
 1 tsp. salt
1 tsp. black pepper
2 loaves frozen garlic bread, 16 oz. size
1 cup shredded cheddar cheese

In a mixing bowl, add the ground beef, croutons, whipping cream, ketchup, onion, Worcestershire sauce, salt and black pepper. Stir until well combined. Separate the garlic bread into halves. Spread the ground beef over the loaves.

Place the garlic bread on a baking sheet. Preheat the oven to 400°. Bake for 20 minutes or until the ground beef is no longer pink. Sprinkle the cheddar cheese over the top. Bake for 5 minutes or until the garlic bread is toasted and the cheese melted. Remove the sandwiches from the oven and serve.

Open Face Garlic Toast Chicken Burgers

Makes 6 servings

2 lbs. lean ground chicken breast
1/3 cup mayonnaise
1 tbs. stone ground mustard
1 tsp. salt
1/2 tsp. black pepper
12 slices Texas Toast frozen garlic bread
Burger toppings and condiments as desired

In a mixing bowl, add the ground chicken, mayonnaise, mustard, salt and black pepper. Using your hands, mix until well combined. Form the meat into 6 patties.

You can grill the chicken burgers or cook them in a skillet. To grill, spray your grill with non stick cooking spray. Place the burgers on the grill. Cook for 5 minutes on each side or until the burgers are no longer pink. Remove the burgers from the grill and let the burgers rest for 5 minutes.

To cook the burgers in a skillet, spray a large skillet with non stick cooking spray. Place the skillet over medium heat. When the skillet is hot, add the burgers. Cook for 5 minutes on each side or until the burgers are no longer pink. Remove the burgers from the skillet and let the burgers rest for 5 minutes.

While the burgers are cooking, preheat the oven to 400°. Place the garlic bread slices on a baking sheet. Bake for 5-7 minutes or until the garlic bread is golden brown. Remove the bread from the oven.

Place a burger on the top of 6 garlic bread slices. Fix the burgers with your favorite toppings. I like to use a southwestern salad dressing on this burger. Place the remaining bread slices over the burgers and serve.

Onion Topped Garlic Caesar Burgers

Makes 4 burgers

1 lb. lean ground beef
2 tbs. chopped fresh parsley
1/2 cup Caesar dressing
1/2 tsp. season salt
4 onion slices, 1/2" thick
4 slices frozen Texas Toast garlic bread
2 1/2 cups shredded lettuce
2 tbs. shredded Parmesan cheese

In a mixing bowl, add the ground beef, parsley and 2 tablespoons Caesar dressing. Using your hands, mix until well combined. Form the meat into 4 patties.

In a large skillet over medium heat, add the burgers. Cook for 3 minutes. Flip the burgers over and place the onion slices over the burgers. Place a lid on the skillet. Cook for 8 minutes or until the burgers are no longer pink and the onion tender. Remove the skillet from the heat.

While the burgers are cooking, bake the garlic bread. Preheat the oven to 400°. Place the garlic bread on a baking pan. Bake for 7 minutes or until the garlic bread is toasted and golden brown. Remove the garlic bread from the oven.

In a mixing bowl, add the remaining Caesar dressing, lettuce and Parmesan cheese. Toss until the lettuce is coated in the dressing. Spoon the lettuce over one side of each garlic bread slice. Place the burger and onion over the lettuce and serve.

Garlic Ranch Cheeseburgers

Makes 4 servings

1 lb. lean ground beef
1/4 cup finely chopped onion
1/4 cup chopped fresh parsley
1/3 cup prepared ranch dressing
1/4 tsp. black pepper
16 oz. loaf frozen garlic bread, thawed
4 slices American cheese, 1 oz. each

In a mixing bowl, add the ground beef, onion, parsley, ranch dressing and black pepper. Using your hands, mix until combined. Form the meat into 4 patties. In a skillet over medium heat, add the burgers. Cook about 5 minutes on each side or until the burgers are browned and no longer pink. Remove the skillet from the heat.

While the burgers are baking, bake the garlic bread. Separate the garlic bread into halves. Place the garlic bread on a baking sheet. Bake for 8 minutes or until the garlic bread is golden brown and toasted. Remove the pan from the oven.

Place the American cheese slices on one half of the garlic bread. Place the burgers over the cheese. Place the remaining garlic bread half over the burgers. Cut into sandwiches and serve.

Veggie Delight Sandwiches

Makes 4 servings

1/2 cup thinly sliced onion
2 cups sliced fresh mushrooms
1 tbs. unsalted butter
1/4 tsp. salt
1/4 tsp. black pepper
8 slices frozen Texas Toast garlic bread
8 green bell pepper rings, 1/4" thick
4 slices colby jack cheese, 1 oz. each
8 thin tomato slices
24 thin zucchini slices
8 red bell pepper rings, 1/4" thick

In a skillet over medium heat, add the onion, mushrooms, butter, salt and black pepper. Saute the vegetables for 5 minutes. Remove the skillet from the heat. Preheat the oven to 400°. Place the garlic bread slices on a baking pan. Bake for 4 minutes. Remove the bread from the oven.

Spoon the mushroom mixture over the garlic bread slices. Place a green bell pepper ring over each bread slice. Cut the colby jack cheese in half and place a slice over each piece of garlic bread. Place 1 tomato slice, 3 zucchini slices and 1 red bell pepper ring over each bread slice.

Turn the oven to the broiler position. Broil for 4 minutes or until the garlic bread is toasted and the vegetables lightly browned. Remove the sandwiches from the oven and serve.

Garlic Bread Grilled Cheese

Makes 4 sandwiches

8 slices frozen Texas Toast garlic bread
8 oz. American cheese, sliced

Preheat the oven to 400°. Place the garlic bread slices on a baking sheet. Bake for 5 minutes. Remove the garlic bread from the oven. Place the American cheese slices over 4 garlic bread slices. Place the remaining bread slices over the cheese.

Bake for 5 minutes or until the cheese melts. Remove the sandwiches from the oven and serve.

Grilled Pimento Cheese Sandwiches

Makes 8 sandwiches

1 1/4 cups mayonnaise
4 oz. jar diced red pimentos, drained
1 tsp. Worcestershire sauce
1 tsp. finely grated onion
4 cups shredded cheddar cheese
16 slices frozen Texas Toast garlic bread

In a mixing bowl, add the mayonnaise, red pimentos, Worcestershire sauce, onion and cheddar cheese. Stir until combined. Refrigerate the pimento cheese at least 2 hours before serving.

Preheat the oven to 400°. Place the garlic bread slices on two large baking pans. Bake for 5 minutes. Remove the garlic bread from the oven. The garlic bread will not be toasted at this point.

Spread the pimento cheese on 8 garlic bread slices. Place the remaining bread slices over the pimento cheese. You will need to cook the sandwiches in batches. In a large skillet over medium heat, add the sandwiches. Cook for 3 minutes on each side or until the bread is toasted and the pimento cheese melts. Remove the sandwiches from the skillet and serve.

Bacon, Garlic & Onion Grilled Cheese

Makes 4 sandwiches

8 slices bacon, diced
1 onion, thinly sliced
8 slices frozen Texas Toast garlic bread
8 slices cheddar cheese, 1 oz. each

In a large skillet over medium heat, add the bacon. Cook for 10 minutes or until the bacon is crispy. Remove the bacon from the skillet and drain on paper towels. Add the onion to the skillet. Saute the onion for 5 minutes. Remove the skillet from the heat and drain off any excess grease from the onions.

Preheat the oven to 400°. Place the garlic bread slices on a baking sheet. Bake for 5 minutes. Remove the garlic bread from the oven. The garlic bread will not be toasted at this point.

Place 1 slice cheddar cheese over 4 garlic bread slices. Spoon the bacon and onions over the cheese. Place the remaining cheddar cheese slices over the bacon. Place the remaining bread slices over the cheese.

In a large skillet over medium heat, add the sandwiches. Cook for 3 minutes on each side or until the bread is toasted and the cheddar cheese melted. Remove the sandwiches from the skillet and serve.

CHAPTER INDEX

Appetizers

Side Dishes & Breads

Garlic Mushroom Stuffing, 19
Garlic Bread Salad, 20
Broccoli Corn Bake, 21
Garlic Parmesan Corn Casserole, 22
Bacon Cheddar Garlic Toast Fries, 23
Cheeseburger Garlic Fries, 24
Garlic Toast Fries With Variations, 25
Layered Garlic Bread Salad, 26
Italian Garlic Bread Salad, 27
Italian Stuffed Mushrooms, 28
Black Olive Herb Garlic Bread, 29
Creamy Garlic Bread, 29
Pizza Pesto Bread, 30
Herb French Bread, 30
Herb Vegetable Garlic Cheese Bread, 31
Cayenne Garlic Bread, 32
Greek Garlic Bread, 33
Mexican Cheesy Garlic Bread, 34
Dill Garlic Bread, 35
Garlic Pesto Bread, 35
Cheesy Bacon Onion Garlic Bread, 36
Sicilian Garlic Bread, 36
Potato Crusted Garlic Texas Toast, 37
Savory Mushroom Toast, 38
Easy Garlic Croutons, 38
Spicy Garlic Croutons, 39
Rosemary Garlic Croutons, 40
Garlic Breadcrumb Mix, 41

Main Dishes & Sandwiches

Main Dishes & Sandwiches, cont'd

Grilled Garlic Vegetable Sandwiches, 81
Fresh Spinach & Bacon Sandwiches, 82
Cheesy Spinach Bacon Sandwiches, 83
Fried Eggplant Sandwiches, 84
Three Cheese Tomato Melt, 85
Baked Turkey Southwestern Sandwiches, 86
Cheddar Guacamole Burgers, 87
Po' Boy Cheeseburgers, 88
Open Face Garlic Toast Chicken Burgers, 89
Onion Topped Garlic Caesar Burgers, 90
Garlic Ranch Cheeseburgers, 91
Veggie Delight Sandwiches, 92
Garlic Bread Grilled Cheese, 93
Grilled Pimento Cheese Sandwiches, 94
Bacon, Garlic & Onion Grilled Cheese, 95

ABOUT THE AUTHOR

Lifelong southerner who lives in Bowling Green, KY. Priorities in life are God, family and pets. I love to cook, garden and feed most any stray animal that walks into my yard. I love old cookbooks and cookie jars. Huge NBA fan who loves to spend hours watching basketball games. Enjoy cooking for family and friends and hosting parties and reunions. Can't wait each year to build gingerbread houses for the kids.

Printed in Great Britain
by Amazon

34865652R00066